Francesco Scolozzi

URBAN SPACES ITALIAN TOWNS

a window to the possibilities

Editor

Francesco Scolozzi

URBAN SPACES ITALIAN TOWNS

a window to the possibilities

Amazon Editor

Acknowledgments

My warmest thanks to the people who have been important in the preparation of this book:

JoAnn Normand for her continuous support in editing the manuscript of this book
Rosalind Cardone Lind who has been specially important in the final editing of the manuscript of this book
Licio Marotta for his assistance during several visits to Puglia
Peter Wang for plans editing
Bob Kalisz for his advice
Planning departments of Bari, Alberobello, Locorotondo, Ostuni, Martina Franca, Lecce, Otranto, Gallipoli for supplying the town maps

Copyright 2022
Francesco Scolozzi
All rights reserved

Photographs by
Francesco Scolozzi

Editor
Amazon

*To Italy, the country of my birth
to my mother and father Candida and Luigi
who inspired and guided me to go further*

Contents

Credits 1

Prologue 8

The influence of cultures and conquests in the making of Italian towns 11

MEDIEVAL TOWNS OF PUGLIA

Puglia a brief historical introduction 22

Bari 24
A brief historical introduction
The seaport city fortress

Alberobello 45
A brief historical introduction
Spontaneous architecture without architects

Locorotondo 56
A brief historical introduction
The white round place

Ostuni 70
A brief historical introduction
The white town

Martina Franca 84
A brief historical introduction
The tax free town with the Baroque twist

Lecce 94
A brief historical introduction
The Florence of the South, Baroque architecture

Otranto 128
A brief historical introduction
The easternmost Roman seaport

Gallipoli 132
A brief historical introduction
The western most Roman seaport

Bibliography 148
Curriculum 149

Prologue

LOOKING INTO THE PAST TO INSPIRE A VISION OF THE FUTURE

In this book, you will encounter a vision of the future drawn from my understanding and appreciation of the complexity of city planning and urban development that comes from a lifetime of passion and love for city planning and architecture. The inspiration is derived from the beauty and harmony of the urban spaces of the past.

With even a modest appreciation of the history of architecture, the reader may find their own inspiration in the picturesque assemblage of public urban spaces, built form, shapes and shadows of the architectural presentation illustrated in the pages of this book.

The Italian region of Puglia, also known as Apulia, was chosen as the setting for "Urban Spaces Italian Towns". Occupying the "heel of the boot", this is the most southeastern region of Italy. In the ancient towns of Puglia pleasing architectural shapes and welcoming urban spaces abound at every twist and turn.

The book is divided into two sections.

In the first section, following a brief synopsis of the missteps of modern city planning, I describe my vision and hope for the expanding and emerging cities of tomorrow.

The reader is then taken on a broad tour of the history, politics, and culture of Italy through the ages. The tour begins with the influence of the Greek City on early Roman architecture and follows through to the time of the Renaissance and beyond. Within this contextual framework, the builders of Puglia are introduced to the reader and I describe how the past influenced the design and construction of their towns.

Through the historical background presented in the beginning pages of the book, it is hoped that the reader will develop an appreciation of the continuous urban development that, from the beginning of civilization, reaches out to us even today as an inheritance from many generations of builders who came before us.

In the second section of the book, the reader will find a detailed presentation of the urban spaces of eight ancient towns of Puglia. Here, the reader is invited to experience the surprise and wonderment that I experienced meandering through the streets and alleyways of this region of Italy.

It is hoped that the many beautiful ancient buildings, the fine balance of form and shapes, and the spatial relationship and harmony that are expressed with imagination and sensitivity throughout the region of Puglia will be as inspiring to the reader as they were to me.

One finds niches carved into walls decorated with flowering plants, flying arches, small and elongated public squares and public courtyards; then a piazza that becomes the focal point at the end of a street. Streets that have been intentionally widened simply for the purpose of making an urban statement. Spaces that flow one into the other as they become the foreground of important civil or religious buildings. Buildings bridging over streets; alleyways framing landscapes. All these and more are found in beautiful harmony in Puglia where they create vibrant living experiences for both residents and visitors alike.

Even in the presence of a towering cathedral or an important civic building, in towns such as are found here, the overall human scale is preserved. In Puglia, individual expression is not found in conflict with unity; rather, one finds a unity without uniformity in the urban fabric, a diversity without fragmentation.

The builders of the past created dynamic urban places for human experience, often resolving challenging problems with ingenuity and creativity and they have much to offer the planners and builders of the modern city.

It is by reclaiming the human perspective of earlier times that the architects and urban planners of the future will find the essence of urban living and the spiritual guidance and inspiration that has often been so elusive in the modern-day quest to improve the design of our cities, communities, and neighborhoods.

Modern times

In recent times, city planners all too often failed to preserve the human scale that is still found in ancient towns. We now live in a very different and unnatural reality, one that increasingly weighs heavily on the human spirit. What are the lessons to be learned from the etiology of the precipitous decline in the quality of life in the modern urban environment?

With the advent of rationalism, beginning in the 20th century, intellectuals began to think that subdividing the city into sections relating to their function would be the exemplification of progress. Cities were divided into agricultural land, industrial areas, office areas, central business and residential districts. Decisions about land use were made without taking into account the concepts of diversity and integration.

As the population of cities grew, the modern urban settlement was increasingly defined by agriculture and industry sprawled out over the landscape well beyond the city core. The historic town centers, where government functions resided, became the point of interchange between the older inner city and the newer agricultural and industrial development on the outskirts. This resulted in the tentacular expansion of the modern city.

Land speculation and new developments outside the political boundaries of the original urban areas contributed to depressed conditions and social dysfunction in many parts of cities. Community functions, often categorized solely on the basis of productivity, were given pretty much the same level of planning priority as agriculture, industry and business. In hindsight, it is not surprising that our cities often failed to develop to their full potential.

As time went on, the creation of the modern urban highway was the solution of city planners in their attempt to reintegrate city functions that had become all too segregated and fragmented during the Rationalism and Post-rationalism movements of the 20th century. This response to the urban/suburban divide proved to be misguided, as it simply gave rise to the further problem of the congested highway.

To the dismay and chagrin of modern city planners, the construction of ever more and bigger roadways did little to resolve the new traffic congestion quandary and many parts of the modern city lost what little remained of their human scale. The modern-day engineering marvel of the multilane superhighways with their multi levels increasing interchanges brought little relief. This effect persists to the present day; during peak hours in modern urban centers all over the world, traffic comes to a standstill and commuters often face longer and longer commuting times.

Since World War II, the increased popularity of the automobile all too often monopolized the attention of urban planners and architects. Regrettably, the roads, highways, and parking lots built in the industrialized world during the post-war period time and again led to the "sterilization" of the urban cores of cities. This was especially visible in North America; it occurred to a lesser degree in Europe and more so in some Asian countries where the North American highway-building model was adopted in a misguided effort to reconnect the increasingly fragmented sections of their emerging cities.

As new urban highways bisects parts of inner cities, they created physical and visual barriers behind which neglected areas suffered from economic and geographic isolation and became slums. A serious degradation of the human, harmonious, sustainable, and eco-friendly environments of the modern city was the inevitable and lamentable result.

I was taking my Master of Architecture in Urban Design at Harvard University when the Central Artery known as "The Big Dig" project, the tunneling of Hwy I-93 crossing Boston's downtown area, was being debated in civic and academic circles. This was the first attempt that I was aware of to address the harm done to the urban fabric of the American cities caused by the highways of the 20th century and gave me reason to hope for a better future, especially for the inner city.

Later, in 1996 I began my architectural practice in China after winning an international competition for the design of the Nanjing Science Centre. I was greatly disappointed and even shocked to see the construction of new highways and multi-level highway interchanges built in the middle of old urban neighborhoods in Beijing and Shanghai. In Beijing, many traditional narrow streets called Hutongs, with their traditional courtyard houses, were being demolished to allow the construction of these new urban corridors and redevelopment of inner-city land for more economical profit. It was only after the objections of several famous international architects that the remaining Hutongs were saved from destruction.

Decades of research have now demonstrated that urban environmental factors can contribute to a variety of pathological, aggressive and even violent behavior in people.

Repetition and monotony in the city fabric can lead to depression, malaise and alienation that in turn become contributing factors to drug abuse and criminality. Surely these were not the intended outcomes of the urban planners of the past.

Statistics show that urbanization is increasing and it is estimated that by 2025 and beyond most of the world's population will live in a megalopolis. This is not necessarily a cause for alarm.

As urban development continues to move forward in the 21st century, architects and urban planners are moving on from a nihilistic epoch of Post modernity and have begun to newly appreciate the importance of the human scale that is still so well expressed in the architecture of historic towns and cities throughout the old world.

Increasingly, human interaction and participation in the politics of city development have opened up new chapters in the revitalization of neglected areas of our modern cities. Hopefully this process will lead to a continued re-emergence of the humanized city.

In many parts of Europe, the old urban centers have once again become vital components of urban life. Many streets and sections of the historical centers have been redesigned for pedestrian and non-motorized transportation use only and with the removal of the automobile from city centers, neighborhood businesses and social life are thriving.

In North America, the revitalization of downtown areas has brought new vitality to neglected neighborhoods. Social activity, walking, shopping and street-oriented businesses have injected renewed life into the city office precinct in the hours beyond the traditional working day.

Cities and new towns will need to continue to expand "Urban Green and Blue Spaces" to improve the quality of urban living and promote a sustainable way of life that will enhance the health and well-being of their residents.

Creative ideas and innovative solutions are required if this new momentum is to be sustained and nurtured. The rehabilitation of existing urban spaces, the new city expansion and the creation of new urban spaces of the future will depend to a great extent on initiatives that are emerging from the lessons of the past.

New technologies such as the computer, the World Wide Web and high-speed land transportation are allowing us to be creative and innovative in ways that were unthinkable or merely the stuff of dreams little more than a decade ago.

While there will be many challenges along the way, one cannot help but marvel at the possibilities that are now emerging around the world as the visions of the future begin to unfold in the urban environments of the 21st century.

The possibilities are limited only by the imagination and ingenuity of the human spirit.

Francesco Scolozzi

The influence of cultures and conquests in the making of Italian towns

The transformation of human settlements

Italy, a country where diverse civilizations and cultural movements merged, is often regarded as the cradle of Western civilization for many good reasons: the Magna Grecia in southern Italy, the Etruscans in what is now Tuscany, the Samnites in the central south part of the peninsula, the Roman Empire extending from Rome to the Mediterranean basin and a good part of Europe, the foundation of The Roman Catholic Church, the Medieval transition, the Renaissance, the Baroque, Neoclassicism and finally the Risorgimento that unified the Italian nation.

For a period of over two and a half thousand years, for better or for worse, Italy was subject to invasions from southern Mediterranean populations, e.g. Greeks, Phoenicians, Saracens, and from northern and eastern Europe when the ancestral tribes of present day France, Spain, Germany and Austria also conquered large areas of the Italian peninsula.

The influence of the incursions by peoples of different cultures had a significant and lasting impact on Italy's city structure and architecture. These influences often persisted and are recognizable in the preserved cultural regionalism that is so prevalent in Italy even to this day.

The Greek city

The Greek city became the model for human coexistence with nature for Italy's early planners and city builders. Here we find the roots of harmony with nature.

Greek city spaces were divided into three sections: a) the residential section occupied by houses, b) the sacred precinct where all the temples were located, and c) the public areas used for commerce, theatre and sports.

Temples and public buildings tended to rise above the city scape and were usually placed, whenever possible, on elevated areas of the natural landscape (Athens Acropolis). The Greek city in its whole form was an artificial organism designed by its planners to respect the surrounding natural landscape by incorporating nature into their architectural statement and design.

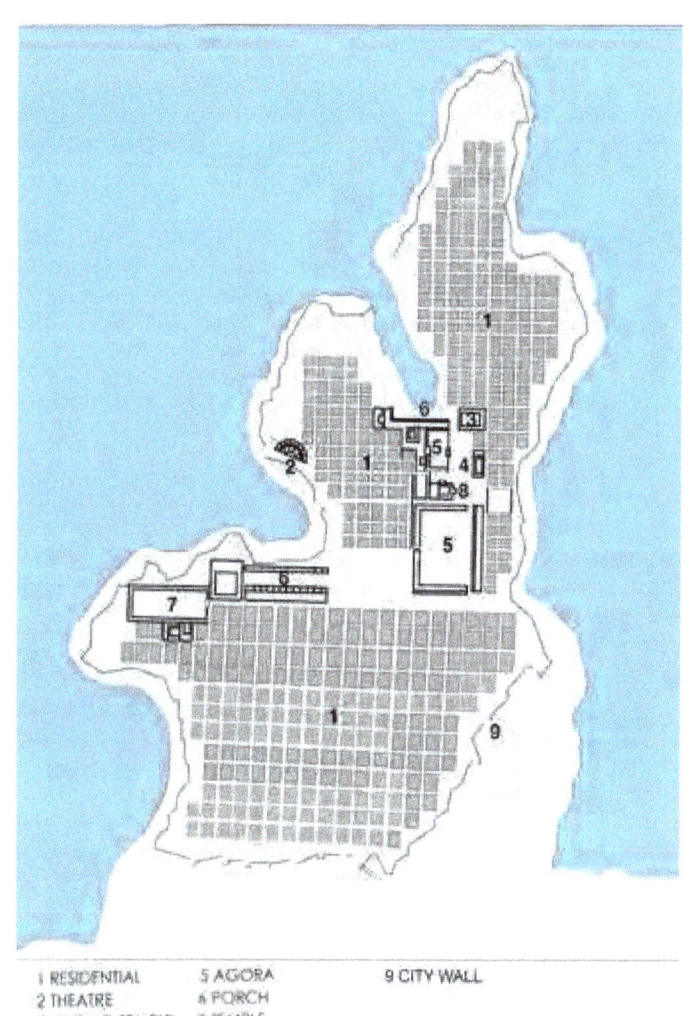

1 RESIDENTIAL 5 AGORA 9 CITY WALL
2 THEATRE 6 PORCH
3 APOLLO TEMPLE 7 TEMPLE
4 GYMNASIUM 8 COUNCIL CHAMBER

The ancient city of Miletus

The Greek city was designed in the form of a geometrical rectangular grid using the Plato ratio "Fye" (1,618) that was applied to both the city scale and the building scale.

Public and religious areas did not obtrude on the city grid but rather, by using a multiple module, they became part of the city grid conformation. Therefore, streets did not cross public areas but were rather tangent to public space. The consistency of the city grid was interrupted only where natural impediments existed (Miletus).

The architecture of the ancient Greeks greatly influenced Roman city planners during the early stages of the Roman empire and this influence is still evident wherever ancient Roman edifices have been preserved.

The Roman city

In a departure from Greek architecture, substantial changes were introduced by the Romans in regional and urban planning, especially in the use of land, the organization of territorial areas, and the development of infrastructures. These changes extended even to the political arena. They included:
- Streets, bridges, aqueducts, the sewage system (Cloaca Massima) and fortifications.
- The division of land for agricultural purposes (Centuriation).
- The creation of new cities
- And the decentralization of political powers.

In their town planning the Romans employed a grid similar to that used by the Greeks. However, the geometrical orthogonal grid, which was considered sacred geometry, was used to create square city blocks instead of the rectangular blocks of the Greeks. The intersection of the two major arteries of the square city blocks, the Cardo Maximus in the north-south direction and the Decumanus Maximus in the east-west direction are recognizable even today, as this is where the Forum was located as well as the basilica, temples, the macellum, i.e. food market, and other important public buildings.

The groupings and placement of temples within the Roman urban fabric involved a range of geometric shapes, e.g.

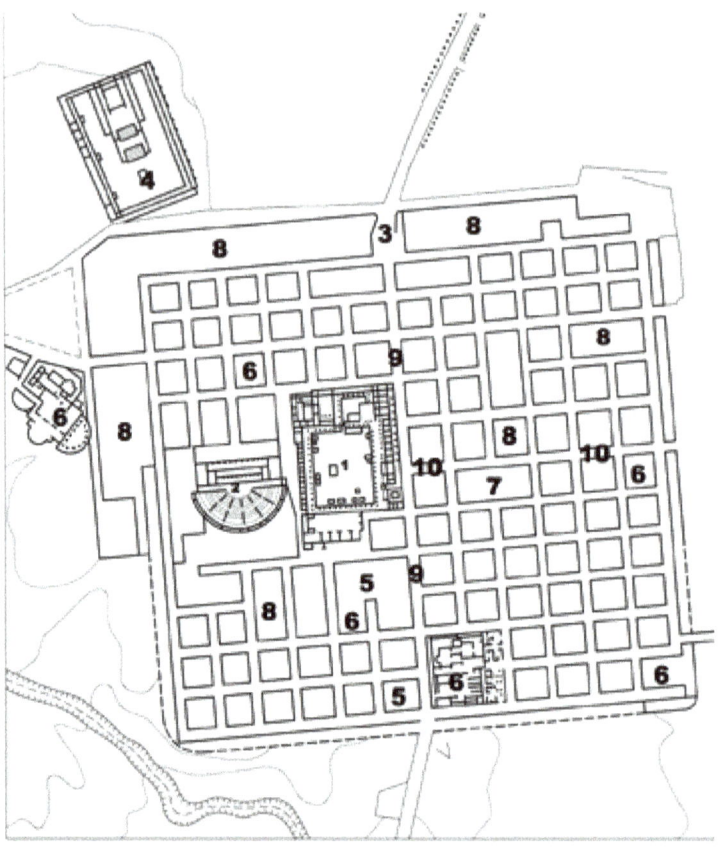

1 FORUM
2 THEATRE
3 ARCH OF TRIUMPH
4 CAPITOL
5 MARKET
6 THERMAL BATH
7 LIBRARY
8 RESIDENTIAL
9 CARDO MAXIMUM
10 DECUMANUS MAXIMUM

Well preserved ancient Roman town of Timgad, (Algeria)

Opus reticolatum

round, elliptical and rectangular, and were located in specific areas of the urban landscape. Of particular note is the elliptical shape of the amphitheater; constructed of stone, it was an entirely Roman creation and was designed to hold up to 80,000 spectators (Colosseum), quite an achievement, even by modern standards.

The state oversaw all aspects of construction and building techniques evolved during Roman times. One of the most significant advancements was the use of "Opus Caementicium", a hydraulic setting cement that incorporated pozzolanic ash. This innovation prevented the formation and spreading of cracks in brick walls. This technological innovation allowed the finishing of walls in what was called "Opus reticulatum"; it produced a very robust diamond-shaped volcanic tuff surface that survives in many ancient buildings to this day. Marble, granite, and travertine were introduced to finish and decorate the interior and exterior of buildings.

For the first time in the history of architecture, the Romans introduced curves in the construction of their buildings. They also used arches and barrel vaults, domes (Pantheon), and semi-domes (Caracalla thermal bath).

Most important in Roman town planning was the variety of institutional architecture that distinguished Roman civilization from the Greek and later from the emergent medieval culture of the Middle Ages. In one form or another, many Roman architectural innovations are still in use today, and they have such a foundational influence that they will continue to find expression in the visions of the planners and architects of the urban environments of the future.

The Medieval city

With the fall of the Roman Empire, between the 5th and 8th centuries A.D., we saw the decline of western civilization and the invasions of northern European and Islamic tribes in the southern parts of Italy. In the wake of the ensuing destruction of many of Italy's ancient towns and cities, living standards dropped precipitously and Roman architecture fell into decline.

This period was, in many ways, the darkest age of architecture in Italian history and brought with it the ruin of much of the harmony and human scale of urban living that was so well manifested in the architecture of ancient Roman cities.
With the invasions came economic crisis and political turmoil, the collapse of the Roman Empire, the ruin of the city, and the exodus of its inhabitants to the countryside where there was a better chance of survival.

Feudalism emerged from this new migration to rural areas and the city became marginalized and less important, consequently could no longer function as the administrative center of society. As time went on, new towns and cities were built on the remains of the old Roman city ruins. Smaller buildings were constructed on the remains of the old city. Compared to the apex of the Roman era, social character, urban planning and building organization were very different.

As time went on medieval urban areas evolved and matured. The new settlements adapted to the natural conformation of the land, for example, hills and the natural setting were used for military defenses and early warning lookouts. Every city had a wall for its defense and as the city expanded other walls were built in a concentric fashion. Existing city walls were often retained and reinforced to protect the city.

The efficiency in the production of materials was of a lower standard compared to that of Roman times. The government kiln, the transportation of foreign marble and the large number of slaves, working inexhaustibly became things of the past. Where public buildings of the Roman civilization remained standing, were transformed into residential dwellings (Teatro di Marcello in Rome) or modified as additional fortifications.

The population that was not working in the countryside settled in the city where they created new economic opportunities in their roles as master craftsmen, guilds, and merchants, thus forming the basis of a new economic and social fabric of the urban areas of the time. New settlements did not exhibit the planning seen in Roman towns and cities. The placement of buildings in the medieval urban space was somewhat arbi-trary, perhaps due to a lack of culture and architectural so-phistication. Since medieval city structure was not clearly defined, any form was possible. A network of irregular streets hence took shape, often on account of the primacy given to the strategy of defense in city planning. There was a hierarchy to piazzas, main streets, secondary streets, alleys, and public dead-end. courtyards.

The city square, or piazza, would come to define large public spaces within the street network. Houses were multi-floor constructions that flanked roadways or piazzas and defined the character of the streets and squares. Important public buildings such as the City Hall, the Feudal Palace, and cathedrals and basilica were, in most cases, located in the piazzas.

Public and private spaces are not contiguous and separate as they were in the previous civilization. There is a public space that is complex, unitarian and adjoining that extends within the urban fabric in which public and private buildings are located, internal functions are facing courtyards and/or private gardens.

Over time, the public spaces of the medieval cities developed a complex character and structure as they served increasingly diverse constituencies such as the religious powers and their fraternities, the municipal government, merchants and artisan guilds, and the castle of the ruler. Tall structures such as the city hall tower, the cathedral dome or the pinnacle of the bell tower were located in the city center and became the landmarks of the city.

Large cities may have had more than one city center and became a privileged urban space where rich and noble families dwelled while the working class lived on the fringes of the city.

The northern invaders of the Roman Empire had the notion that art was an expensive obligation and consequently, unlike in Roman time, art was not extensively commissioned for civic buildings. The exceptions were the religious edifices such as the cathedrals dedicated to Mary or devoted martyrs that became the focal point of the city's special celebrations. Baptisteries were located in proximity to the cathedral or basilica while secondary churches were built for daily services and were distributed throughout the city.

Stone architecture and architectural structures such as vaults remained in use but were reduced in size and did not have the same level of refinement as in Roman civilization. What remained from the Roman ruins, columns, capitals and stone blocks, were reused in the construction of buildings and churches. Medieval architecture had little to no correlation with the Classical architecture of ancient Rome.

The sense of unity in the plans, facades, massing, interior and exterior spaces of the Christian Basilica was intended for religious services in contrast to the Roman basilica that was the site of legal and business matters.

Medieval Italian towns continued the use of stone and or bricks in the construction of houses according to the local availability of raw materials. The medieval house varied from city to city. It was the evolution of centuries of urban living and thus changed over time.

With the emergence of the medieval economy based on crafts, guilds and commerce there was a revival of Roman building typology. The ground floor of city buildings were once again allocated to shops or crafting workshops, while the above two or three storeys were reserved for residential use. The shop owners and craftsmen used the second floor for its family dwelling (piano nobile), the upper floor was for workers and apprentices, and the attics was reserved for storage.

Houses were built contiguously along the perimeter of the city block. The front, facing the street, could have an arcaded portico in stone or wood as in northern Italian towns. Large courtyards in the interior of the city blocks were subdivided according to the peripheral plot sizes and would contain stables, orchards or smaller courts where garments were washed and hung to dry. Since the town size was limited, the plots were narrow with tall adjoining houses.

The Renaissance city and its artistic culture

The new way of thinking about architecture and city planning began in Florence where the rich families patronage: Pazzi, Pitti and Medici led the way to a new direction in art and architecture.

The rise of Florence in prestige and power redefined the new way of life and began with its support for the arts. **Arnolfo di Cambio, Donatello, Botticelli, Ghiberti, Masaccio, Verrocchio, Filippo Lippi, Paolo Uccello** and **Brunelleshi** surged to fame by rediscovering the forgotten legacy of Greek and Roman art and architecture. The relics of Roman architecture, sculptures and frescoes were studied and measured to understand the essence of design, the principles of harmony and proportion that was the intrinsic nature of classicism.

Filippo Brunelleschi, (1377-1446) was called to design and supervise the construction of Santa Maria del Fiore, Florence's cathedral, the Ospedale degli Innocenti, San Lorenzo Church, the Cappella Pazzi, the Santo Spirito Church and several other buildings. All these works exhibited the new expression in architecture.

Brunelleschi redefined the new approach to architecture by producing in advance, drawings and precise preconstruction models. All decisions regarding the design were made to define the proportion and the relationship of detail to the overall construction. The drawings were produced with dimensions, construction materials were selected during the design process and defined where they were to be used.
The components of a building such as columns, trabeation, arches, vaults and other architectural components had to conform to the models established by Roman Classicism.

Humanists like **Leon Battista Alberti,** (1404-1472) were searching for documents that described the greatness of classical architecture. Alberti studied the Roman architect and Planner **Marcus Vitruvius Pollio's** "De Architectura" a description of the human body proportion and the perfect proportion in architecture (Plato). Alberti, was a theoretician of architecture and planning and wrote "De Re aedificatoria", which became "the manual" for all Renaissance architects. His important works were Palazzo Rucellai and the church of Santa Maria Novella in Florence.
Architecture acquired a cultural and intellectual significance and was elevated to the level of visual and liberal arts.

Other architectural theoreticians followed in Alberti's footsteps.

Antonio di Pietro Averulino Filarete, (1400-1469) designed Sforzinda (1465), a new town for Francesco Sforza, Duke of Milan.

Francesco Di Giorgio Martini, (1439-1470) wrote the " Trattato di Architectura, ingegneria e Arte Militare ". A visionary of architectural theory, his third book was entirely dedicated to city planning, proposing the polygonal geometry. Siena's Dome was architectural masterpiece.

Sebastiano Serlio, (1475-1554) published the "Five books of Architecture".

Giacomo Barozzi Vignola, (1507-1573) designed great works of architecture and published "Regola dei cinque ordini d'architettura", describing his interpretation of design proportion of the five orders of Roman architecture.

Vincenzo Scamozzi, (1548-1616), architect and planner, designed the new fortified town of Palmanova for the Republic of Venice. Palmanova's plan diverges substantially from that of any previous city or town's planning. The geometry is an nonagon with nine streets converging in a hexagonal central square. Access to Palmanova is through three gates connected to streets approaching from the northeast, northwest and south.

Andrea Palladio, (1508-1580), whose work in the late Renaissance, was one of the most influential, international and the most famous architect in the history of architecture, he wrote "I Quattro libri dell'architettura".
First book
Is an analysis of materials and techniques that lists five classical orders: Doric, Ionic, Corinthian, Tuscan and Composite.
Second book
Analyzes and describes the design of urban houses and countryside villas
Third book
Dealt with city planning, streets, bridges and piazzas.
Fourth book
Organized in five chapters, describes the Roman temples of antiquity and contemporary church design.

The Renaissance approach to town planning and building design swept across the Italian peninsula and into Europe. The masters of the Renaissance introduced an inspiring new direction in architecture and the arts. This new architecture became a remarkable addition to the medieval urban fabric.

The aristocrats' palaces, the dome or cathedral within a proper setting would elevate the importance of a street and town's prestige. Street enlargements and piazzas were creatively carved into the medieval town allowing the construction of remarkable buildings that have passed into the history of architecture as monuments.

Important buildings were placed as focal point at the end of streets or built where streets were enlarged. In some cases buildings were set with skew to the axis or placed at the end of a square, or surrounded by a square (Milano's Duomo, Santa Maria del Fiore in Florence). In every town there is a different solution depending on the urban pre-exhisting conditions. The new illuminated approach to architecture and planning did not result in any major restructuring of the city. The demographics of the medieval towns stabilized toward the middle of XIV century and there was no need, with few exceptions, to expand or create new towns.

Renaissance governments and the governing nobility that replaced the communal governments and the territorial monarchies had neither the political stability nor the wealth to subsidize ambitious restructuring or expansion of the towns.

Puglian towns followed the architectural revolution of the Renaissance but could not afford the services of the great Renaissance masters. Local architects studied the great masters of Florence and Rome and consciously applied to their work the new principles of design and replicated in their ownbuildings the new standard of architecture.

Transformations in the city's morphology were made to accommodate these prominent new buildings with attention and respect to pre-existing urban spatial structure in almost every city of Puglia towns.

Baroque culture and growth

As the Renaissance period ended, the Scientific Revolution, which began in the early XVII century marked the beginning of modern science that influenced the changes in the direction of urbanism and architecture.

With few exceptions, the new ruling class, the nouveau riche, the bourgeoisie and the church, following the Catholic Reformation did not have the same ambitions as in the previous century. Works of architecture lost objectivity and became more subjective. This was the reaction to the conformism of classical architecture.

No substantial changes were made in the urban fabric of Puglian towns, however many Baroque public buildings have enriched the urban spaces of those southern towns. Street enlargements and new squares were made clearing part of the old urban fabric to accommodate baroque buildings and churches. The great changes in Urbanism occurred in the larger cities and capitals of Europe.

PUGLIA

MEDIEVAL TOWNS OF PUGLIA

Puglia a brief historical introduction

Puglia has a rich historical past which is quite unique on the Italian Peninsula. Subject of many invasions from foreign powers to acquire the strategic location it occupies on the East Mediterranean sea.

The ancient name of Puglia was Apulia, it has a rich archeological past. It was colonized by the ancient Greeks "Magna Grecia" with its own architectural expression.

First populated by an indigenous tribe called Iapigi. Sannites, originating in Umbria and the Messapians (from the east Adriatic sea), settled in the southern part of Apulia. It was occupied by the Carthaginians and subsequently conquered by the Romans. Puglia was an important trading route for the Romans with the eastern empire.

Puglia was and still is an important center for the production of grain, oil and wine. In 1059 the Duchy of Apulia was formed by the Normans, and became the center of the Norman em-pire under Robert Giscard. During the 12th and 13th century the German King Frederick II "Red Beard" occupied the re-gion and several castles were built for its defence. Castel del Monte built in 1240 is an octagonal shaped building situated in the northern part of Puglia and is a unique masterpiece of Medieval architecture.

Towards the end of the 13th century Apulia became part of the Kingdom of Napoli under he House of Anjou and subsequently the House of Aragon and afterwards by the Bourbon nobility, It was part of the Kingdom of Sicily.

Puglia was raided by Ottoman pirates and became the battleground between the Venetians and the Ottomans who alternatively occupied parts of coastal Apulia. From the 12th until the 17th century beautiful picturesque hilltowns and coastal towns were built for its defence. Many of the watch towers and castles still standing today are in excellent condition. Puglia was under the Austrian empire from 1700 to 1735 then went back under Spanish Bourbon domination until 1806. It was conquered by Napoleon Bonaparte and governed by Joaquin Murat until the unification of Italy in 1860.

The historical center of Bari, Alberobello, Locorotondo, Martina Franca, Ostuni, Lecce, Otranto and Gallipoli have memorable layers of history and a complex urban structure with interesting architectural styles.

Polignano a Mare coastline

BARI

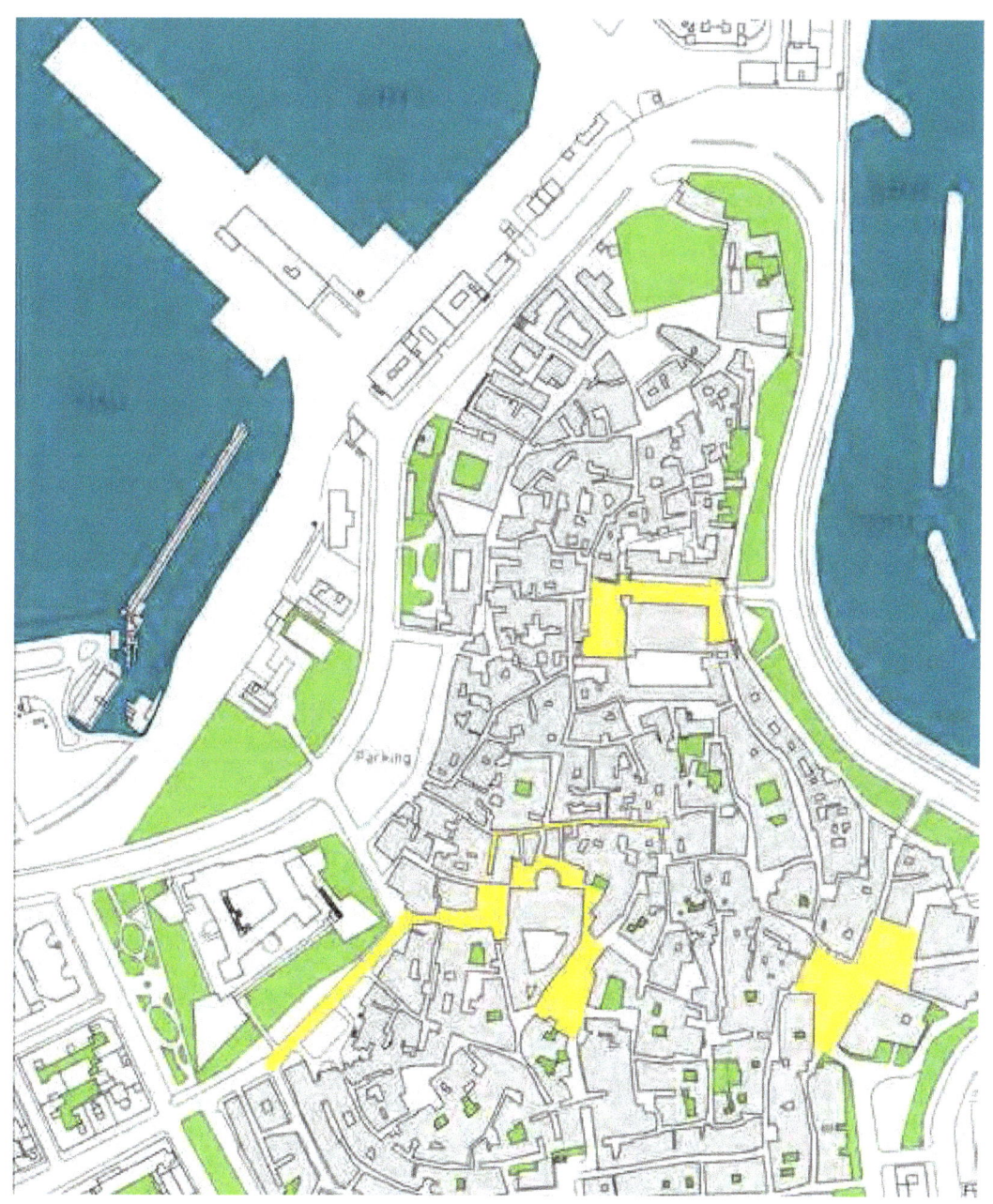

BARI
A brief historical introduction

Every "Barese" will tell you "everyone was here," meaning that over the course of its history many peoples from old Europe and the Middle East have settled for some time in their city.

The history of Bari reaches back 3-4,000 years. In 1913 the archeologist Prof. Michele Gervasio discovered the remains of a prehistoric village in the proximity of Piazza San Pietro.

During the XVI century B.C. the Illyrian tribe of the Balkans, invaded Bari, followed in the 11th century B.C. by the Messapians (coastline Balkans) and later by the Greeks at which time Puglia became part of Magna Grecia.

From the III century B.C. to the IV century A.D., Bari was under Roman domination and the port became an important trading center. The Romans made the city a "Municipium," which allowed it to have its own laws and institutions. The "Barium Municipium" still paid taxes to Rome and depended on it for military support.

By the middle of the IV century A.D. the Roman Empire was weakening. The Goths (eastern Germans), Visigoths and Ostrogoths (branches of the Goths) had an important role in the fall of the western Roman Empire. King Flavius Theodoricus, of the Ostrogoths conquered Italy and Puglia and remained in Bari until the middle of the V century. Justinianus Augustus, Emperor of the Eastern Roman Empire, also known as the Byzantine Empire, defeated the Ostrogoths and Puglia remained under the Byzantine domination until the middle of the VI century.

From the middle of the VI century to the middle of the VIII century the Longobards, a people from southern Scandinavia, defeated the Byzantines and occupied Italy and Puglia.

The city of Bari had been assaulted by the Saracens since the early XI century. From 847 to 872 Bari was under siege by the Saracen. The Longobards allied with the Byzantines defeated the Saracens and it remained under the Byzantine Empire until the end of the X century. In the year 1002 the Saracen army attempted to conquer Puglia once again and was defeated by the Venetian Doge Orseolo II.

Byzantine domination ended in 1071 with the conquest of Bari by the Norman King Robert Giscard who became Duke of Puglia, Calabria and Sicily. During this time the relics of San Nicola (Saint Nicholas) of Myra (Turkey) were taken to Bari and temporarily deposited in the Monastery of St. Benedict. They were moved to San Nicola's Basilica upon its completion in 1197.

Bari was an important center for the congregation of the First Crusade army of western Europe for the conquest of the Holy Land.

The Norman dynasty had no male successors consequently Constanza d'Altavilla of Normandie married the Swabian king Henry the VI of Hohenstaufen. Frederick II, successor of Henry VI, restored the Bari castle. In 1268 Charles of Anjou conquered southern Italy and Bari went under Anjou domination. The city was neglected by the new conquerors and fell into one of its darkest periods.

In 1442 the Kingdom of Naples and Bari were ruled by Alphonse V of Aragon. In 1464 Bari was given to the Sforza family for helping the Aragons during the succession war. Isabella of Aragon married Galeazzo Sforza Duke of Milan and became the Duchess of Bari. Under Isabella, Bari reached a new splendor. The castle was restored as we see it today. Bona Sforza, daughter of Isabel and wife of Sigismund I of Poland, succeeded as Duchess of Bari. She died in 1557 and her mausoleum is in San Nicola Basilica.

After Bona Sforza's death Bari was reannexed to the Kingdom of Naples and entered into another period of neglect until its resurgence in 1713 under Charles VI of Habsburg.

In 1734 the Kingdom of Naples returned under domination of the Spanish Bourbon King Ferdinand IV. In 1799 Bari elected a revolutionary government and in 1805 Napoleon Bonaparte occupied Bari. Napoleon's brother Joseph Bonaparte was declared King of Naples and later was succeeded by Napoleon's brother-in-law, Joaquin Murat in 1808. Bari again entered a period of prosperity and expanded beyond its city wall. The district of Murat was built on a rectangular city grid and began to take shape.

After the fall of Napoleon in 1815 Bari returned under the government of Ferdinand II of Bourbon. He was succeeded by his son Francis II who was deposed in 1860 by the Italian unification movement. Bari and Puglia became unified with the other regions of Italy under Victor Emmanuel II, King of Italy, ending 3,000 years of foreign domination.

The Seaport City Fortress

The city of Bari is divided into two sections. The old medieval section, which the Baresi call "Bari Vecchia," between the old port on the east side and the new port on the west side of the city. The new section is the expansion under Joachim Murat. On the east side of the old town, behind the Basilica San Nicholas exists a part of the old city wall that extends to the southeast in proximity of Piazza Ferrarese.

The unusual triangular shape of the old town is attributable to the fact that it follows the shape of the peninsula. Medieval cities were usually built on the ruins of previous civilizations. Important buildings were rarely retained until the Renaissance awakened the consciousness of society to the importance of keeping its glorious historical past. Roman monuments and plans were studied to discover the principles of proportion and composition. Vitruvius, in his ten books titled "De Architectura," describes the principles of city planning and architecture and Renaissance builders developed their own principles of proportion (Golden Section) and city planning.

The medieval city is an elaboration of the precinct that excludes the surrounding exterior space and isolates a limited interior urban fabric. The interior urban fabric, a rich and intricate arrangement of narrow streets, is a place for human experience. It varies in form and space and is the framework of individual expression in which the entire community participates.
Significant structures such as the early Romanesque (architectural style of Medieval Europe), the Basilica of San Nicholas (1197) with its surrounding square and the Romanesque San Sabino Cathedral (1292), with its Moorish motif dome, dominate the urban space and are located in the center of Bari Vecchia.

Piazza San Nicola and Largo Papa Urbano II form an L shape that surrounds San Nicholas's Basilica, similarly to Piazza Dell'Odegistria facing the cathedral. The enlargement created by Strada Ronchi which surrounds the Cathedral and the Bari archdioceses on the south side constitutes a diversion in the compactness of the old town's narrow streets. The visitor can appreciate the beauty of these two splendid examples of Romanesque architecture. These enlarged spaces would accommodate public congregations or religious ceremonies.
On the left of the old city, facing the new Port of Bari, is the Norman Swabian castle built by King Roger around 1132, later destroyed in 1156 by the Sicilian King William I and rebuilt by Frederic II of Hohenstaufen. It was modified by Ferdinand of Aragon and subsequently given to Bona Sforza.

The castle is surrounded by a moat on three sides. The north side is flanked by the Adriatic Sea and on the south side is the entrance gate and the bridge over the moat. The tower is what remains of Frederic II's construction while the castle walls are part of the Aragonese restoration and reinforcement. The construction appears powerful and monolithic, articulated in two sections, one atop the other. It has a large court at its center.

On the east side of Bari Vecchia are two large squares which face the old port. Piazza Mercantile has been the center of administrative and commercial activities since the 14th century. The square is surrounded by important architectural statements: the 16th century Sedile Palace, headquarters of the Nobles Council of Bari, the 16th century Dogana Palace, the Baroque fountain and the "Column of Infamy," where insolvent debtors were tied to the column and exposed to public pillory.

Piazza Ferrarese took the name of a 17th century Ferrara businessman who moved to Bari and owned several buildings in the square. The square is defined by an 1840 building which houses the fish market and the Vallisa Church. In the foreground the boulevard Emperor Augustus faces the Adriatic sea and the old port.

St. Nicholas Basilica (1087-1197)

Piazza San Nicola
The King Anjou gate (1340) at the center of the picture. The Pilgrims porch on the left side of the Moorish influenced Anjou gate. At the center of the photo is St. Gregorio's Church (XI century D.C.)

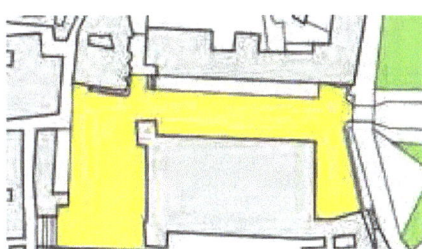

Lions portal detail (1197)

Interior of St. Nicholas

The central nave of St. Nicholas church

St. Nicholas and Adeolato, paintings by Carlo Rosa (1661-67)

Norman Svabian Castle entrance gate and bridge, (1131)

Norman Svabian Castle southeast view

The castle tower is the western focal point of Piazza Dell' Odegitria

St. Sabino Cathedral (XII-XII century) is the eastern focal point of the square

San Sabino Cathedral's bell tower

window masterpiece of puglian sculpture, end of XII century

St. Sabino portal

Piazza Bisanzio e Rinaldo

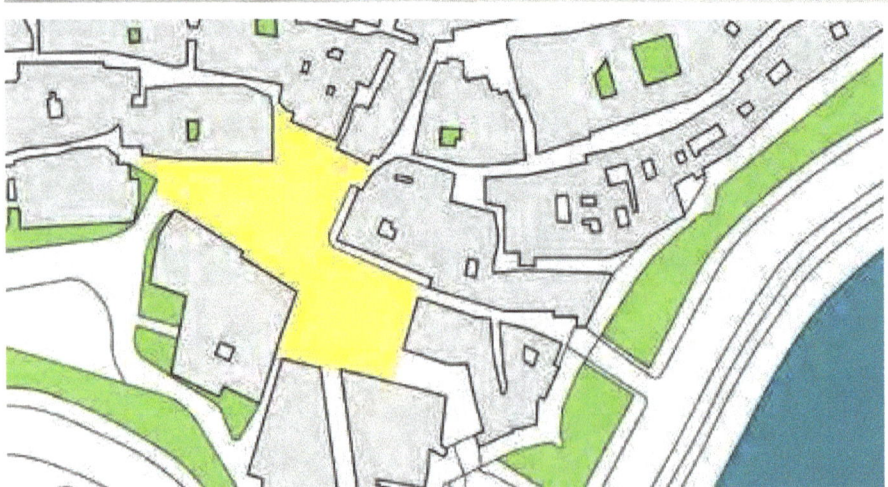

Palazzo del Sedile, (1446) on the West side of Piazza Mercantile

Colonna dell' Infamia

Vicolo della Neve

Arco delle Meraviglie XVII century

Courtyard in Via San Luca

Santa Teresa dei Maschi, (1696)

ALBEROBELLO

ALBEROBELLO
A brief historical introduction

Situated in the Itrian Valley, the town derives its name from the Latin, 'Silva arboris belli" woodland of beautiful trees. Alberobello is famous for its dwellings called "Trulli". The homes were initially of a typical cylindrical shape and later evolved into buildings with a more squarish base topped with conical roofs. The style of these buildings is very ancient and dates back to the prehistory of the Itrian Valley. Similar dwellings exist in the Balearic Islands, Ligurian Alps, Ireland, Cameroon and Kurdistan.

Alberobello lands were granted to Count Andrea Matteo Acquaviva in 1481 by Robert of Anjou, King of Naples as a reward for his father's service in the battles to retake the port city of Otranto, which had been captured by the Ottomans. His father, the late Count of Conversano, lost his life in the effort.

Alberobello remained a fiefdom of the Acquaviva family until 1797. King Ferdinand IV of Bourbon freed it from feudal servitude, making it a royal city, part of the kingdom of Naples. Joachim Murat, Napoleon's brother-in-law, was crowned King of Naples and succeeded the Bourbon domination. The Bourbons retook control of the kingdom of Naples in 1860. Alberobello became part of the kingdom of Italy in 1861.

Spontaneous Architecture without Architects

The best examples of trullis are in the "Monti district" located on the south side of Alberobello, a UNESCO World Heritage site. The picturesque town scape is quite unique in the Itrian Valley; the Rione Monti consists of five streets configured in a funnel shape. Via Monte Santo, Via Monte Sabotino, Via Monte San Michele and Via Monte Nero depart from Largo Martellotta and rise toward the top of the hill. The best view of the Rione Monti is from the stairway that connects Largo Martellotta to Piazza Plebiscito.

Around 1000 A.D. several villages of this nature were established. The earliest existing trulli dates back to the 14th century. The walls were built directly on bedrock; two parallel layers of stone without mortar were filled with soil to achieve good insulation. The wall thickness varies and in some cases reaches 3 meters which explains the comfortable temperature in summer as well as in winter.

The conical roofs were constructed with staggered rings of limestone called 'chiancarelle' and were topped with stone pinnacles of various shapes, thus was the signature of the master builders.

The construction is of stone layers assembled without a bonding agent so that the dwellings could be easily disassembled. It seems that this was an expedient way to avoid royal taxes imposed by the Bourbons. The exterior stone walls were originally not plastered. The exterior plaster finish must have been introduced later when the tax issue was somehow resolved and the trullis became permanent residences. The exterior plaster was whitewashed to reflect the intense heat of the sun.

The amazing aspect of the trulli is the way in which it was planned; it is a combination of nature and invention, an articulation of organic forms. It is an aggregation of "cells" that were added as the family needs arose and varies from one building to another. The juxtaposition of open spaces and private orchards enhances the harmonic creation of forms and sculptural shapes. The steps leading to the roof are an integral part of the walls. Exterior seating can be seen carved into some of the exterior walls, the fireplace chimney and roof were built as a harmonious whole. The intense south light, shining on the white walls and shadows of the agglomerated cells contrasts beautifully with the deep blue sky.

The inner space within the trulli cluster contains the old orchards that still exist today. One is presented with a fascinating and unforgettable picturesque scenography that varies at every corner as you move along the winding streets and is a delight to the visitor.

Rione Monti
The streets of Rione Monti have a special character. Straight and sinuous alleys enlarge and shrink to create a picturesque neighborhood unseen in larger cities

Spontaneous "germination" of spaces reflects the patriarchal family character Alberobello

Christian and zodiacal or religious symbols adorn the conical roofs

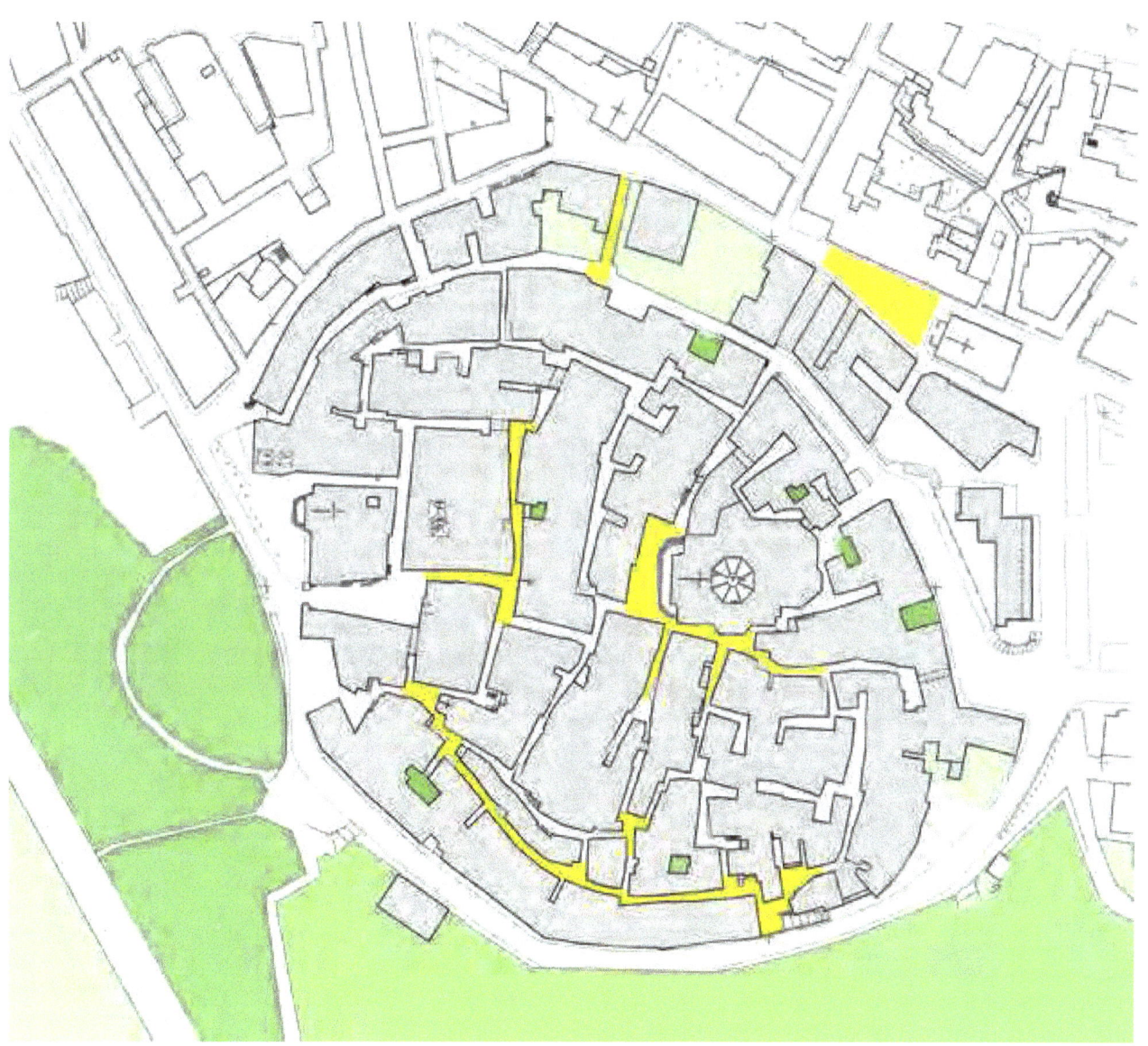

LOCOROTONDO
A brief historical introduction

The name "Locus Rotundus" derives from the 13th Century Latin. There is no precise information on its origin, however information from archeological sites dating from the 7th to the 3rd centuries B.C., suggests that a Messapian population lived in this area.

The town was presumably founded around the XI century A.D., as indicated in a document from the Benedictine monastery of St. Stephen in Monopoli. The name of the town has changed several times but has always reflected the settlement's round shape. Locorotondo meaning "round place."

Locorotondo's Middle Ages' history is linked to events in other cities and towns of Puglia. After the fall of the Roman Empire (476 A.D.), Locorotondo was invaded by the Goths (488-493 A.D.), the Longobards (668-847A.D.), the Saracens (847-872), the Byzantines (876-1071), the Anjou (1268-1442) and the Aragons (1442-1458).

During the 15th century Locorotondo became part of the Kingdom of Taranto, governed by Orsini Del Balzo. Subsequently, in the middle of the 18th century, it became part of the duchy of Francesco Caracciolo. The Habsburgs ruled from 1713 to 1734 and the Bourbons from 1734 to 1798. It was part of the Kingdom of Naples under Joaquin Murat and was unified with the rest of Italy in 1861 under Victor Emmanuel II.

The White "Round Place"

Locorotondo a well known beautiful hill town and in certain ways is quite similar to Ostuni. Its round shape minimizes the extent of the city wall needed in defence against aggressors.

The medieval historical center is located on the south side of the modern town. The best approach to the town is from Via dei Templari named after the Templars, (a military order of Catholic knights founded during the Crusades), where it is possible to admire the whitewashed houses built in concentric rings bracing the hill. Their unusual pitched roofs, called "Cummerse," are a unique character of Locorotondo's architecture. The cupola and the bell tower of St. Giorgio Cathedral emerges above the ring of white houses.

From Via dei Templari looking up towards the city wall, it is possible to admire the man made stepped hill where the medieval orchards were once located.

Locorotondo's urban typology is typical of medieval town buildings conceived by bridging over alleys as a means to detect and defend against approaching invaders. The urban fabric is a labyrinth of white narrow streets, dead ends, articulated alleys, staircases and bracing arches, houses built upon houses. Street enlargements were made in proximity of important buildings such as the Baroque Cathedral of St. George the Martyr to allow religious gatherings.

The old castle was presumably located between the funnel shaped Largo San Rocco that faces the Church Santa Maria della Grecia and Piazza Victor Emanuel II. Piazza Victor Emmanuel II was enlarged during the late 1800's to celebrate the unification of Italy and its new ruler. The best access to the piazza is from "Porta Napoli," where two columns from the old town gate remain.

The aristocratic Palazzo Morelli built during the 18th century is a very interesting example of late Baroque architecture. The elaborate stone portal, embellished with the family crest, windows and balconies with cornices all carved out of warm ochre sandstone contrasts nicely against the whitewashed walls. The balconies have beautiful intricate iron work.

St. Giorgio's Cathedral emerges from the exterior ring of whitewashed houses

The Locorotondo hill was terraced with local stone to create the orchards

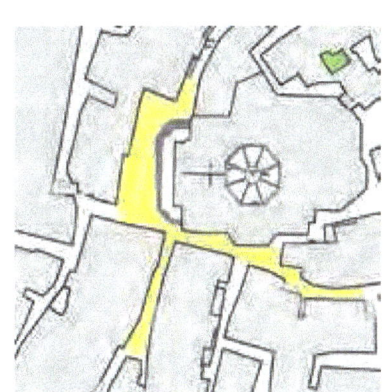

Piazza Rodio, St. Giorgio Cathedral
(1790-1825)

Largo San Rocco and stairway to Via Vittorio Veneto

The chapel Madonna del Soccorso (1627-1632) is the focal point of Largo Soccorso at the instersection with Via Regolo

Flying buttresses frame the alley and brace the buildings on the opposite sides

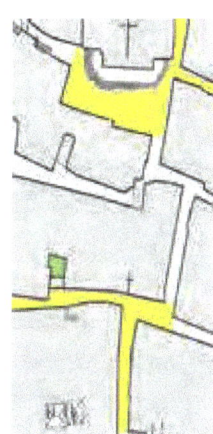

Via Bruno

Palazzo Morelli beautiful stone artwork and ironwork frame the main entrance and balconies

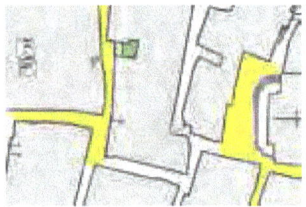

Locorotondo countryside

OSTUNI

OSTUNI
A brief historical introduction

The site which Ostuni now occupies was a Messapian settlement destroyed by Hannibal during the Punic Wars between Rome and Carthage (264-146 B.C.). The Greeks rebuilt on this site when they settled in Magna Graecia (Puglia) and they named it Asty Neon which means "New City."

The Greeks were succeeded by the Romans and the city remained under Roman domination until the fall of the Roman Empire in 448 A.D. It was then occupied by the Ostrogoths followed by the Longobards. In the 9th century the town flourished under the Normans and several new buildings were erected including the castle which was later demolished by order of the Duke Zevallos.

During the 16th century Ostuni was governed by Isabel of Aragon, Duchess of Bari, wife of Gian Galeazzo Sforza, Duke of Milan. This was Ostuni's renaissance period. After the death of Isabella her daughter Bona Sforza, wife of Sigismund I of Poland, continued Isabel's legacy by building fortifications along the shoreline to defend against the Saracens. The city fell under Spanish Bourbon domination until the unification of Italy in 1861.

The white town

Ostuni and Alberobello are considered the jewels of spontaneous Mediterranean architecture in Puglia. Ostuni is a typical example of a Mediterranean settlement; its whitewashed buildings are situated on the slopes of the Murge plateau a few miles from the Adriatic Sea. Public buildings such as churches and portals of prestigious family palaces are built using pink and light brown sandstone that creates a nice contrast against the white. The cathedral encompasses Romanesque, Byzantine and Gothic elements of architectural heritage from previous occupations.

Approaching the town from afar, the two limestone monumental Baroque churches, the Cathedral San Maria Assunta and San Vito Martire (now a museum of pre-classical civilization) contrast dramatically with the white town scape. The construction of the town was articulated in a series of rings built approximately on the same elevation and connected by sloping and narrow stepped streets. Staircases and arches cross alleys connecting buildings on opposite sides. Dead ends and unexpected small gardens open to glimpses of the Adriatic sea, the valley and the bright blue sky.

The oval shape of this town was perhaps chosen, as opposed to a square shape, to help in reducing the perimeter of its fortification. The original Messapian wall was restored and completed during the Aragons reign and is today preserved almost intact. Houses have expanded into the city wall and openings have been carved out to bring light into the living quarters.

The town was planned in consideration of its climate and strategic principles of defence. Its roads are tortuous and articulated with enlargements, dead ends and houses facing each other and bridging over alleys. This would have made it difficult for invaders to succeed in occupying the town. To maximize building space no town squares were constructed but later some streets were enlarged to accommodate public gatherings for special occasions.

Walking along Viale Oronzo, the ring road which runs around the town wall, you can see how the hill was modified with a retaining wall, built of local stone. The slope changed into a stepped configuration allowing the formation of orchards for the town's inhabitants.

Ostuni was build with lots of imagination and a certain local sensibility. Architectural forms pierce the sculptural walls and surfaces to create a variety of loggias, balconies and stairways all in a continuous harmony and dynamic balance. The systemization of irregularities adapted to the sites brings a contrasting relationship and a dynamic tension that is resolved with imaginative solutions.

There is a stunning and picturesque view of the town as one approaches from the east through Contrada Rosara. The intense light and shadows cast by architectural forms make every twist and turn of the narrow streets a surprise and delightful experience. The town has harmony and a strong sense of community and is almost entirely pedestrian. There is a sense of peace and joy living in an environment where pollution, dust and noise are almost non-existent.

Approaching the town from the southeast

Residences are incorporated into the city wall as a whole

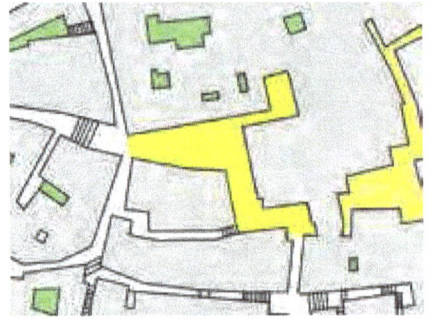

Santa Maria Assunta's cathedral (1228-1229)

Piazza Giovanni Paolo

Piazza Spennati

Via Duomo

Vicolo Spennati

Multilevel access to the town are incorporated into the urban fabric

Residences bridge across the alleyway and flying buttresses become part of the urban landscape

Town levels interconnected by stairways

The ancient noble class is identified by the family crest above the doorway

Southern view ot Ostuni. Santa Maria Assunta's Cathedral and San Vito's Martire dominates the stratification of white houses

MARTINA FRANCA

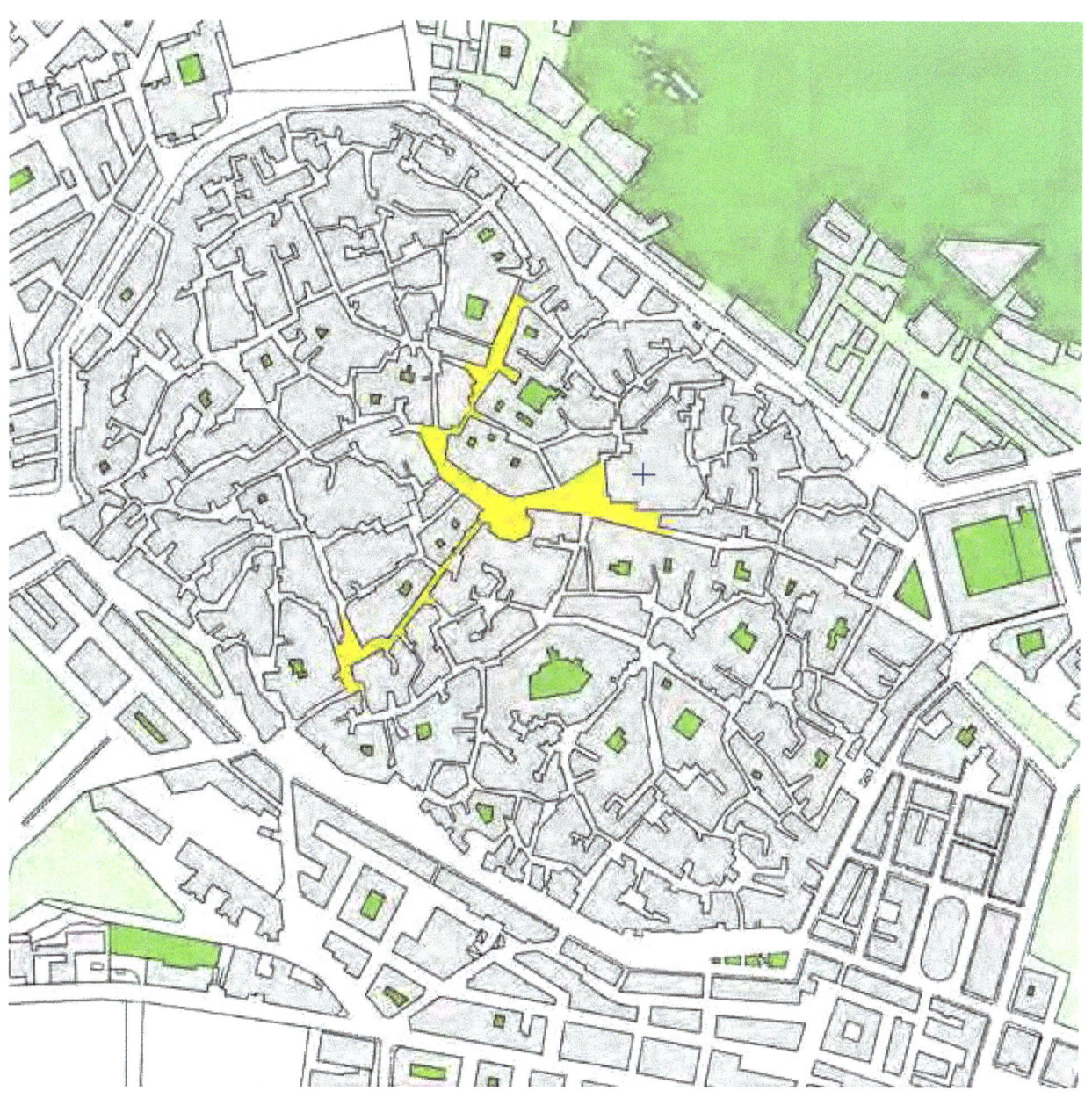

MARTINA FRANCA
A brief historical introduction

Martina Franca, a hilltop town, was founded between the 9th and 10th centuries A.D. by people fleeing the coastal cities of southwest Puglia during the Saracen invasions.

The old section of the city (its round shape recognizable on the map), was probably built around the 9th century. The town's name is derived from "Martina", in honour of St. Martin, protector of the city, and "Franca", the Italian word for "free," reflecting the 1310 decree by Philip of Anjou declaring the town tax-free to encourage people in settling there.

Martina Franca was surrounded by a city wall which had twenty-four towers. Under the governance of the Roman Orsini family, the city expanded and a castle was built. In 1668 the Caracciolo family constructed the ducal palace, now the town hall, which was built on the remains of the old castle.

The town wall and towers existed until the unification of Italy in 1861 at which time they were demolished to allow for the town's expansion. Several town gates, Porta San Stefano, Porta San Nicola, Porta San Pietro, Porta Santa Maria and Posteria still remain as do several Baroque and Rococo buildings which enhance the architectural heritage of this prosperous town.

The tax-free town with the Baroque twist

The round shaped historical section is bounded by Via Principe Umberto, Via Conte Ugolino, Via Machiavelli and Via Dante located in the northwest side of the actual town on San Martino hill, the highest of the Murge Plateau. Its winding alleys and narrow street system is typical of medieval towns. Street enlargements allow people to gather for celebrations in front of the Basilica and other important buildings.

Martina Franca has, as other towns of Puglia, an infinite combination of harmony and irregularities. The complexity of the old town's physical urban environment with its alleys and squares that shape the old town enhances important monumental buildings. In subsequent centuries the medieval spaces were enriched with layers of geometrical forms in the Baroque style.

The town is an aggregate of buildings of varying styles where the architecture of a given period can be compared easily to other styles of subsequent centuries. These architectural works have been intentionally designed to be heterogeneous. They were built using different processes and materials such as warm colored limestone which would give it a extended life in comparison to the whitewashed plaster or stucco finish of other buildings.

A stunning example of Baroque architecture is the San Martino's Cathedral, Borromini inspired architecture, located in Piazza Plebiscito. The piazza is triangular in shape and flows into Piazza Santa Maria Immacolata where a 1854 building designed in the Neoclassical style by the architect Davide Conversano makes an architectural statement. It is an elliptical-shaped building with an arcade on the lower floor called "I Portici". This is Martina Franca's "salotto" (living room), Walking from Via Giuseppe Garibaldi to Piazza Maria Immacolata the elliptical arcade presents itself as a scenographic stage set where locals convene for a cafe or gelato.

Another good example of architecture is the 1746 church of San Domenico in a floral Baroque style. Some buildings have their own sense of continuity between the interior (nave, courtyard or interior garden) and the exterior ornate facade. All these architectural components are geared towards the public space by means of a bivalent element that is the facade. This brings light into the interior space while serving as the gateway to the building's interior and presenting the building to its surroundings.

The historical town center of Martina Franca is also noted for a few beautiful Baroque buildings. The Orsini Palace which became the Caracciolo Duke's Palace in 1668, the Nardelli Palace located in Piazza Roma and the Ancona Palace are considered to be some of Martina Franca's finest civic buildings.

Piazza Plebiscito east view. The Baroque Basilica of San Martino (1747-1785)

Piazza Plebiscito west view, a glimpse of Piazza Santa Maria Immacolata

Piazza Santa Maria Immacolata and " I Portici". In the background the Basilica of St. Martino in Piazza Plebiscito

Via Garibaldi the "I Portici" building designed by the Architect Davide Conversano is the focal point of the street

Via Principe Umberto

The Baroque Church of San Domenico

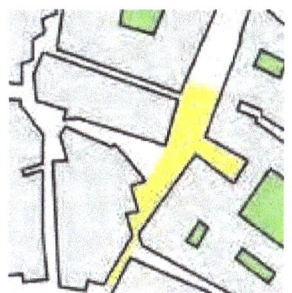

Piazza Roma and Palazzo Ducale Orsini-Caracciolo (1388-1668)

Porta Santo Stefano gateway to Piazza Roma

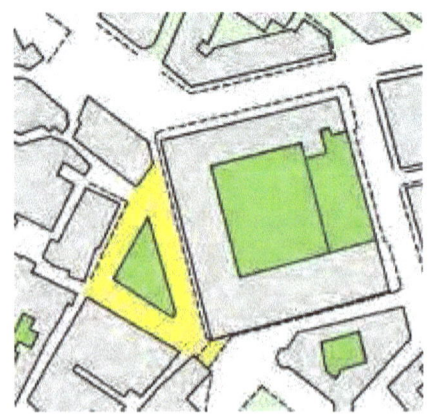

Aristocratic palazzo

Palazzo Fanelli

Vicolo Cavour

LECCE

LECCE
A brief historical introduction

Lecce derives it's name from the city's crest, which depicts a wolf under a "leccio," (Holm tree). It was first named Sybar by the Messapians and subsequently Lupiae by the Romans before its final name, Lecce.

Lecce became a very important center of Puglia during the reign of the Roman Emperor Hadrian, 90-85 B.C. He built the amphitheater located in the historical city center and the road that connects the city to the port, 11 km away. Under Marcus Aurelius, Lecce experienced further expansion and became a prosperous commercial vibrant trading center with Middle East.

After the fall of the Roman Empire in the 4th century A.D., the city fell under the dominance of the Normans who further expanded its commercial influence. Geoffrey of Bouillon had his court in Lecce and it became the most important center in Apulia.

Frederick II of Hohenstaufen, followed by the Anjou and subsequently the Orsini family governed Lecce as it became an influential center of arts and culture.

During the Spanish domination under Charles V, King of Castile and Aragon, a decree was issued to build a castle in the old city center in close proximity to the Roman theatre, the architect was Gian Giacomo d'Avaya. A new city wall was built as a defence against the Ottoman raids.

The economy further flourished under French occupation, headed by Joaquin Murat, brother-in-law of Napoleon (1806-1815). After the fall of Napoleon, Francisco II of Bourbon returned to rule Puglia until 1860 when Lecce and the Salento peninsula (southern part of Puglia) were annexed to the Kingdom of Italy in 1861.

The Baroque architecture of Southern Italy

The XVII and XVIII centuries were Lecce's golden period and the town became the center of Baroque art for the Salento peninsula. For this reason Lecce is known as the Florence of the south. Most of the Baroque buildings we can admire today were built during this period. Lecce's Baroque architecture is unique in the history of Italian Baroque and one can recognize the influence of Spanish Baroque.

Lecce's ornamental Baroque architecture differs from the Baroque of central and northern Italian cities in the creation and exploration of new architectural expressions. The use of distinct theatrical, picturesque, scenographic, exuberant expression of elaborate decorations representing nature, animals, mythological and sacred subjects, overlaps on the architecture of the buildings.

All this was possible because the local warm golden colored sandstone was easy to carve and readily available. The aristocratic residences, churches and many of the less common buildings contribute considerably to the ambiance of Lecce Baroque style. This brilliant architectural trend is on permanent exhibition in Lecce's squares.

Piazza del Duomo and Piazzetta Santa Croce are the best examples of Lecce's Baroque scenographic architecture. Unfortunately many of these beautiful monuments are in danger of being irretrievably lost and damaged by acid rain if the stone is not treated against pollution.

Part of the Roman amphitheater still remains in Saint Oronzo Square beside the Cathedral and Palazzo del Seggio that was built by order of Pietro Mocenigo, Venetian Doge and Admiral of the fleet that defeated the Turks in the Battle of Shkodoer (Scutari) in 1474.

The city fabric that we see today in the old city center is mostly medieval. A ring road separates the historical city center from the modern expansion that occurred after 1890.

Roman Amphitheater and Palazzo Del Seggio (1592) to commemorate Doge Pietro Mocenigo's victory over the Turks in the Battle of Shkodoer (Scutari 1474)

The Roman amphitheater and St. Maria della Grazia, Piazza St. Oronzo

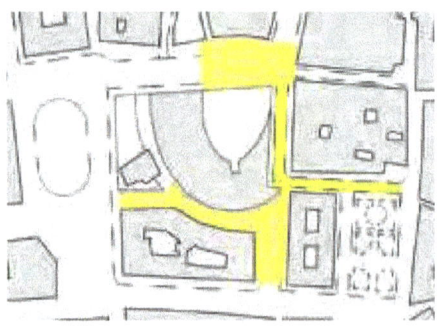

Palazzo del Seggio built by Doge Mocenigo

Gateway to Piazza Duomo

Piazza Duomo

Piazza del Duomo and the Cathedral of Santa Maria Assunta (1144 -1659)

Architectural details of the Bishop's residence,

Via Federico Aragona

Vicolo dei Protonobili

Vicolo Boemando

Palazzo Castromediano

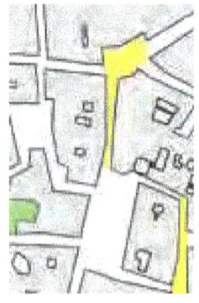

Via dei Conti di Lecce

The Baroque church of San Matteo (1667), designed by Achille Larducci nephew of Francesco Borromini

Santa Croce (Holy Cross) basilica (1582-1606) is the central focus of Piazzetta G. Riccardi

Piazza Santa Croce

Santa Croce Basilica in Piazza Santa Croce

Santa Croce Basilica, a glorious example of Lecce's Baroque architecture, constructed by the architect Francesco Zimbalo, completed by Cesare Penna

Portal by Francesco Antonio Zimbalo 1606

Piazza R. Orsini, Corte dei Pandolfi

To the left, cupola of the Santa Croce Basilica

OTRANTO

OTRANTO
A brief historical introduction

Otranto, named Hydrus by the Greeks, part of Magna Graecia. During the Roman Empire, Hydruntum its subsequent Latin name, was the most important port on the Ionian Sea surpassing Brundisium (Brindisi) in trade with the Eastern Roman Empire.

Otranto experienced a period of great prosperity during the Byzantine domination at which time the Church of St. Peter and the Abbey of St. Nicholas of Casole were built. In 1086 A.D. the city was stormed by the Norman King Robert Guiscard. Otranto became the port where the Crusaders reunited to retake Jerusalem.

The city was fortified by a powerful city wall and castle. One hundred towers were scattered along the coast to sight invading fleets and aid its defence.

On August 11, 1480 a large Turkish fleet attacked Otranto and after 15 days of siege the Turks managed to penetrate its defences and conquer the city. The following day 812 Otranto citizens, who had refused to convert to Islam, were executed on the hill now called the "Hill of Martyrs".

In 1481 Pope Sixtus IV summoned a crusade to free Otranto. King Ferdinand of Aragon organized an army led by his son Alfonso along with the troops of the Hungarian King Mathias Corvinus defeated the Turks who ultimately abandoned the city.

During Napoleon's occupation of southern Italy, French troops were garrisoned at Otranto to spy on the movements of the English fleet. After the fall of Napoleon the Bourbons returned to rule Otranto until 1860. In 1861 Otranto and the Salento Peninsula were annexed to the Kingdom of Italy under Victor Emmanuel II of Savoy.

During World War I the Otranto channel was the theatre of naval battles between the allied Italian, French and British fleets against the Austro-Hungarian fleet. In 1940, during World War II, the Otranto channel was once again the scene of a fierce battle between the British and Italian fleets.

The Eastmost Roman seaport

The medieval portion of the town is located beside the old port on the east side of the town's expansion. The historical center as well as the remains of a powerful wall that surrounded the old town have been preserved. Colorful historical layers of Byzantine, Norman and Aragonese architecture makes the town historically interesting.

There is perhaps more of a sense of history here than in other towns of a similar age where the urban fabric has preserved its medieval origins. The alleys and streets are more spacious and generous than in other towns and picturesque street scapes abound.

Piazza Basilica and Via Duomo surround the Romanesque Cathedral dell' Annunciazione which is graced with well kept XII century floor mosaics. The cathedral was consecrated in 1088 by the Norman bishop Guglielmo on the remains of a Roman villa. After its destruction by the Turks it was rebuilt in 1481. The Baroque portal and the beautiful 16 spoke wheel window above the portal were added later. Surrounded by charming small piazzas and two alleys is the Byzantine Basilica of St. Peter which is embellished with frescoes of the same period.

The 15th century Aragon castle was designed and rebuilt in 1485-98 by Alfonso II to withstand southern invaders. Many factors, previously unknown, influenced the design, their system of defence and the construction of the fortification.

The fortification needed to be able to resist assaults from more powerful war machines. The introduction of gun powder and steel projectiles increased potential damage by canons. This stimulated the architects to design walls capable of resisting greater impacts. The castle's plan is irregular with three powerful cylindrical towers: on the north, west and south sides and a diamond shaped bastion on the east side. The diamond shaped bastion was facing the sea and its triangular shape would deflect the canon's steel projectiles. The round towers provided a defence from an inland attack. The castle is surrounded by a moat and the original plan had a single entrance with a draw bridge.

The Aragonese Castle was destroyed in 1067 and rebuilt in 1222 by Frederic II. During the Turkish invasion of 1480, the castle was partially destroyed and rebuilt by Alfonso of Aragon in 1485-98

Otranto's town wall

Cathedral of St. Maria dell'Annunciazione (1068)

Piazza Basilica

Skeletons of martyrs slaughtered during the Turk invasion of 1480

Baroque 16 spoke wheel window was added in 1674 together with the portal.

Mosaics dated during 1163-65 executed by Pantaleone

Byzantine fresco of Santa Maria dell'Annunciazione

Piazza Basilica south side

Via Basilica

Byzantine church of St. Pietro, built at the beginning of IX century

Via Francesco Zurlo

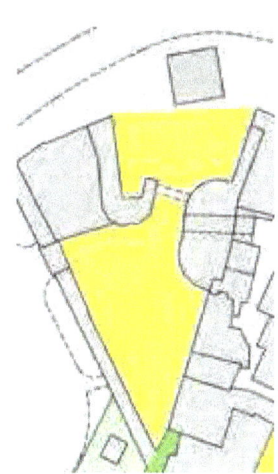
Gateway to Borgo Antico

Largo Porta Alfonsina

Otranto town wall

GALLIPOLI

GALLIPOLI
A brief historical introduction

Founded by the Messapians and named Anxa, it was subsequently, according to legend, occupied by the Greek Idomeneus in 1111 B.C. and named Kallipolis, which means "beautiful city."

The Romans conquered Gallipoli in 265 B.C. They expanded the port connecting the city to the trade road and Gallipoli became a strategic military and trading port due to its position on the Ionian Sea. A fortress was built to house the 7th Roman Legion in the location where the castle exists today.

When the Roman Empire fell in 476 A.D. Gallipoli was invaded by the Ostrogoths. In 554 the Byzantines defeated the Ostrogoths and occupied the city until 688, during this time the castle was restructured and reinforced. The Normans defeated the Byzantines in 1132 and took over the city.

In 1265, Charles I of Anjou occupied Gallipoli and destroyed a good part of the city in vindication of the betrayal of the barons who supported the Swabian king. Charles Anjou, nephew of Robert, helped in its reconstruction. Later Gallipoli was dominated by the Spanish Aragons, during this period there was an increase in crafts and commerce. The economy flourished further and trade made Gallipoli an important port on the Mediterranean Sea.

The Spanish Bourbons succeeded the Aragons and Gallipoli became part of the Kingdom of Naples. Ferdinand I of Bourbon introduced sweeping improvements to the town including reconstruction of the port. Gallipoli became part of the Kingdom of Italy in 1861 under Victor Emmanuel II.

The island fortress

The town was originally sited on an island on the Ionian Sea. The island was connected to the mainland "Borgo" quarter in 1837 by the seafront road Lungomare Marconi and by the 17th century bridge Papa Gianni Paulo II. The Anjou Castle and the old port are on the east side of the island. The old port is between the cape and the island and the north side is defined by the 19th century bridge.

Gallipoli's strategic location and climatic conditions relating to the prevailing winds were taken into consideration during its planning. The alleys and streets are narrow, creating shaded areas and resulting in a difference of temperature from the sun-exposed areas. This allowed for cross-ventilation. The lanes and streets are also winding, winding and articulated to facilitate ambushes making it more difficult for invaders to occupy the town.

In order to maximize building space within the city walls squares were omitted. Several years later some areas were enlarged to accommodate public for special civic and religious events. The main intersection of the Roman city planning "Cardo" (North and South oriented road) and "Decumanus" (East and West oriented road) where the Roman Forum existed, is recognizable in the Via Duoma (Street-Square) where the Basilica of St. Agatha, designed by Giovanni Bernardino Genovino was built in 1629. The facade of the Basilica, completed in 1696 with the warm local stone is a very nice example of Baroque architecture.

Another interesting example of Baroque architecture is the facade of the Church of St. Francis of Assisi which is located in the west part of the town. The church was built in the XIII century and was extensively renovated during the Baroque period by the architect Mauro Manieri. The entrance was modified by the addition of a grand archway with side pilasters and a recessed facade above it. The square in front of the church is a later addition.

On the north and east sides of the island are the remains of the powerful city wall built by the Byzantines and reinforced by the Angevins. The Aragons built the magnificent castle on the remains of the Byzantine fortress where two round towers were added on the north side and a polygonal tower was added on the south side.

In 1522, King Alfonse of Naples commissioned Francesco di Giorgio Martini, a well-known military architect, to design and build the eastern bastion "Rivellino" which protrudes into the canal on the east side of the castle achieving better visual control of the sea from both sides of the island.

The Aragonese Castle was built during the 13th Century, was rebuilt by the Angevin King Alfonso of Aragon and completed in 1522 by the addition of the Rivellino designed by the architect Francesco di Giorgio Martini.

The Rivellino is the new addition to the Aragonese castle

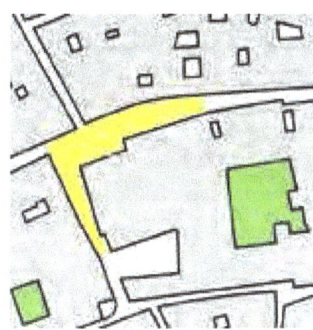

Via Duomo Cattedrale di St. Agata
(1629-1696) by Giuseppe Zimbalo

St. Agata Cathedral's facade detail

St. Agata Cathedral's facade

Via Garibaldi

Santa Maria Court

Via Sant'Angelo

Via Santelia

Chiesa di San Francesco

Via Ribera

Greek fountain approx. 3rd century B.C.

A vision of the future

"Per Gnaritas Ad Astra"

The time has come for the harmony and humanity found in ancient towns and cities, be given serious consideration and inspiration in the planning of future urban spaces.

My recent visit to Puglian towns has been a source of inspiration to me and what the planning of new cities and towns of the future should aspire to. The human scale of the old cities, the awareness of space, the perception of destination in the placement of urban spaces creates a setting for prominent buildings and generates the dynamic for a harmonious spatial event that involves a complete range of feelings.

The awareness of space that engages our sensations, is missing in today's cities. They are somehow anonymous, directed by a hierarchy of circulation systems and addressed to building design neglecting the human scale. The architectural form of the buildings relating to its sites are lacking richness and variety and do not contribute to the character of the city.

I am not suggesting that by reclaiming the human scale in the design of present-day cities can be accomplished by replicating the cities of the past. It would be anachronistic to put aside our culture and advancements and naïve to think that simplistic solutions are the answer to the design of cities of the future.

After a lifetime of experience in the field of urban planning and architecture, I put forward the notion that the city of the future should be planned to use the concept of what I call the "mega city block" wether it's a new town or city expansion. In 2009 we used this idea in the design of Longwangtang master plan, located in the Sakura district of Dalian (China).

The goals and objectives in achieving the best living conditions for the inhabitants of this mega block are:

- Provide a unique sense of place and identity

- Introduce the concept of "Work, Live and Play" (mixed development). Office buildings are located in proximity to the Gateway, the highway access to the community

- We Introduced a large varied housing typologies

- We introduced the Vertical Urban Farming (multi storey green house) to supply green vegetable and fruit to the new community

- We orient the buildings south to achieve the best sun exposure and views of the mountain, river and ocean

- Enhance the existing natural setting by introducing the landscaping concept of a "Garden Community"

- Maximize pedestrian access and circulation

- Enhance pedestrian and bike activity by creating a net work of pedestrian paths linking neighborhoods - an entirely pedestrian promenade is flanking the river and con nects to the Gateway and the Sakura gardens

- Connect the community to Dalian public transit

- Provide storm management for the entire site

- Environmental stainability

- The Sakura garden is the recreational centerpiece of this development

LONGWANGTANG MASTER PLAN

1. Vertical urban farming
2. Shopping mall gateway to Sakura garden

The China Lab Charrette formed by Columbia University, Hong Kong and other Chinese institutions were working at developing a very similar concept during this same period. This gave us the confidence that our planning philosophy was on the right track in the design of future cities and city expansion.

For the most part, the high cost of land and lack of open spaces for new development has made high density unavoidable in urban planning. When densification is not done at its best it can be perceived as one of the most negative aspects of the modern city, however the issue of urban sprawl and its effect on the environment leaves us with few alternatives.

Central to the idea of the **mega bloc** (let's think of a microcosms is the concept that green spaces and high rise and low rise development can coexist to create sustainable healthy neighborhoods that embody the sense of human scale achieved in early historic towns and cities. The **mega block** will do away with specialized zones such as the Central Business Districts of the modern era where financial activities are concentrated in a few city blocks; instead, all human activity will be fully integrated across the new mega block urban space.

Fortunately, more than at any other time in human history, new construction materials and technologies are available to help us achieve such a vision.

The importance of ecology in the modern urban environment can no longer be ignored by the city planners and developers of the **mega city block**. From the outset, the eco-cities of tomorrow will demand a commitment to **global sustainability**.

This ecological commitment will entail new initiatives such as the following, many of which are already in their infancy in parts of the world:

- **Renewable energy, geothermal heating, solar and wind electric generation, and the phasing out of fossil fuels**
- **Work Live and Play (WLP) developments, to reduce commuting time and traffic congestion**
- **Gravitational Control (GC), Magnetic Levitation (Mag lev) or personal drones may become the private and public transportation that would eliminate air pollution while providing fast, efficient, and affordable public transportation to all high density areas of the city.**
- **Upgrading of railways to super high speed GC to inter connect cities and geographic regions to reduce the carbon footprint of air transportation**
- **Urban Diversity with Urban Green and Blue Spaces (UGBS) indexed of to a minimum of 1500 square meters per inhabitant to create a more natural, harmonious, and ecologically balanced living environments for all people**
- **Vertical Urban farming (multi storey greenhouse) that will produce, in a controlled environment, a large variety of fresh and more nutritious fruits and vegetables at lower cost reducing transportation,**

A few further thoughts:
Mixed-use buildings can be located at the edges of the mega city block in proximity to the urban highway. Extensive green spaces, as an integral part of low-rise developments, would bring the harmony of human scale to the neighborhood.

Expanded facades of high-rise buildings can contain extended double skins on their southern exposures where hydroponic urban farms can be developed. Additionally, greenhouse farming can be done on roofs.

Multilane urban highways should have large green buffers separating them from urbanized areas and incorporate large green central areas to allow for future expansion without encroaching on the green buffer.

The Work, Live and Play (WLP) concept, already seen long ago throughout Greek, Roman and Medieval civilizations, can be re visualized in modern terms and applied to all areas of the **mega city block**.
Even as we move beyond the current pandemic era, the shift to remote work that was made possible through high-speed internet and video-conferencing will continue to expand and will connect all the Work Live and Play areas of the **mega block**. In many cases, commuting will be greatly reduced as more people will be working from home.

The brief list of innovations characteristic of the mega city block noted above is far from exhaustive; it is presented here simply to make a few suggestions. While many of them are already being put into practice by today's urban planners in their design in the expansion of existing cities and on the development of new urban areas many other exciting discoveries, ideas, and visions for tomorrow's new urban spaces undoubtedly lie just beyond the horizon.

Now, as you read further, I invite you to discover your own inspirational moments and a vision of the future.

Bibliography

G.C. Argan: The Renaissance City. 1969
R. Auzelle: Enciclpédie de l'Urbanisme, Paris. 1950
N.E. Bacon: Design of Cities, London. 1967
L. Benevolo: The Architecture of the Renaissance. 1978
L. Benevolo: Storia della città, Laterza. 1982
M. Berestford: New Towns of Middle Ages. 1967
V. Bianchi: Ostuni. 2010
L. Bonoldi: Bari 2009
F. Brown: Roman Architecture. 1965
G.A. Bruker: Renaissance Florence. 1975
F. Castagnoli: Orthogonal Planning in Antiquity. 1971
Civitas Europea, Various authors: Principi e Frome della Città, Libri Scheiwiller, Milano. 1953
S. Codarini: Gallipoli, Kale Polis, la città Bella. 2014
K.J. Conant: Caroloingian and Romanesque Architecture. 1966
C. De Seta, I. Insolera: le citta nella storia d'Italia, Roma. 1980
C.A. Doxiadis: Architectural Space in Ancient Grece. 1981
F. Fiore: Places in Puglia Lecce the Baroque town. 2015
F. Fiore: Places in Puglia, Martina Franca 2015
F. Fiore: Places in Puglia, Alberobello and the truly houses
F. Fiore: Places in Puglia, Ostuni the White City
Mimmo Castellano: La valle dei trulli, 1964
S. Giedion: Space, Time, and Architecture. 1967
F. Granger: Vitruvius on Architecture vol. 1 & 2
E. Guidoni, A Marino: il Seicento. 1979
E.A. Gutkind: Urban Development in Italy and Grece London. 1969
S. Kostof: History of Architecture. 1985
P. Lavedan: Histoire de l'urbanisme Paris. 1952
P. Lavedan, J.Huguenay: l'Urbanisme au Moyen Age. Genève. 1974
L. Lavin: Bernini and the Crossing of St. Peter's 1968
B. Lowry: Renaissance Architecture. 1962
M. Lyttelton: Baroque Architecture in Classical Antiquity. 1974
A. Martellotta: Valle D'Itria. Alberobello, Cisternino, Ceglie, Messapica, Locorotondo Matina Franca, Ostuni 2008
H.A. Millon: Baroque and Rococo Architecture. 1961
L. Mumford: The City in History. 1989
P. Murray: The Architecture of the Italian Renaissance. 1963
C. Norberg, Schulz: Baroque Architecture. 1971
L. Patruno: Bari vecchia. 2000
F. Perrini: Valle d'Itria. 2012
P. Portoghesi: Rome of the Renaissance. 1972
L. Puppi: Andrea Palladio. 1986
F. Repishti, R. Schofield: Architecture e Controriforma. 2004
P.G. Ruggiers: Florence in the Age of Dante. 1964
H. Saalman: Medieval Cities. 1968
A. Tzonis, L. Lefaivre: Classical Architecture the Poetics of Order,.1968
J.B. Ward, Perkins: The Cities of Ancient Greece and Italy. 1974
J.B. Ward, Perkins: Roman Architecture. 1988
J.B. Ward, Perkins: Roman Imperial Architecture. 1981
R.E. Wycherley: How the Greeks Built Cities. 1963

- **Jian Shi:** Floating Blocks and the Loss of Urbanity
- **Edward Denison:** History Lessons in Shanghai
- **Eric Chang:** Who's Afraid of the Superblock
- **David Bray and Jun Jiang:** Michael Hulshof and Dean Roggeveen in These Gates Provide Freedom where they explore "whether the megablock (concept inhina) ... could be exported globally as a prototype for theplanning of cities in the future."
- **Dr. Dickson Despommier:** The vertical farm. 2010

francesco scolozzi

Francesco Scolozzi was born in Italy

Education and teaching

- Received his "Magna cum Laude" Doctor in Architecture from the Faculty of Architecture in Florence, Italy
- Received the Master of Architecture in Urban Design from Harvard University, USA.
- Assistant professor at the Faculty of Civil Engineering, Bologna and Florence (Italy).
- Assistant professor at the University of Toronto, Faculty of Architecture and Landscape Architecture.
- Visiting lecturer at Dalian University of Technology, Faculty of Architecture

Private practice of Architecture

- 1967-1976 Vice-director of Architectural magazine "Chiesa & Quartiere".

- In 1968 established my office of Architecture in Bologna; was Consulting Architect for the public developer Finanziaria Fiere of Bologna when Kenzo Tange was appointed to design the Master Plan of Bologna North and Fiera District. Mr. Scolozzi was part of the design team that worked with Mr. Tange on the project.

- In 1976 I Emigrated to Toronto Canada, open my practice and taught architectural design at the University of Toronto.

Awards

- In 1996 I was awarded first price for the Nanjing Science and Technology Building and established my practice in China.
- In 2005 I won the international competition for Dalian Foreign languages University
- Finalist in the international competition for the tennis and hockey stadium, Beijing Olympics 2008
- Recipient of many other international competition awards in China and Canada

www.ingramcontent.com/pod-product-compliance
Lightning Source LLC
Chambersburg PA
CBHW051331110526
44590CB00032B/4477